MICHAE

THE
PLAY

COLLINS COLOUR CUBS

ELTON Woofit had a dog called Gershwin. Gershwin was a most unusual dog because he played football. He was a very good footballer indeed.

He quite liked to play in goal, springing this way and that, and stopping the ball with his front paws. But most of all he liked to play centre forward.

He would run along, controlling the ball with his nose, and showing the most tremendous skill.

The only trouble was, Gershwin couldn't shoot. Elton often thought that if only Gershwin could kick a football, he would be the first million pound dog on the transfer list.

Elton used to take Gershwin for walks on the field where The Woofits team played.

Sometimes they would stop and watch the team practising under the stern gaze of Cluff Woofit, the manager.

No one knew more about football than Cluff Woofit. Elton believed this because he had heard Cluff Woofit say so more than once.

Sometimes, instead of watching The Woofit football team training, Elton would have a game with Gershwin.

While he ran with the ball at his feet, Gershwin would run alongside, waiting for a chance to nose the ball away.

Once Gershwin got the ball, there was no stopping him. He could certainly move, turning the ball from side to side to avoid Elton's tackles. In the end, Elton would have to call him to heel to get a kick.

Gershwin thought this was cheating!

One day, while they were playing in the field, they were spotted by Cluff Woofit.

"By gum! your dog's a good 'un!" said Cluff, who always spoke his mind. "If my players could dribble like that I'd be certain to win t'Cup on Saturday."

The Cup Final was a big day for The Woofits Football Club. They were playing their old rivals, The Cloggers, and it looked like being a very tough match.

"I wish I could play for you on Saturday," said Elton.

"Not this Saturday, son," said Cluff. "Maybe one day . . . . Anyway, why don't you come to the match on Saturday as our mascot?"

Elton was pleased – and Gershwin was pleased because Elton was pleased, and wagged his tail like mad.

Cluff Woofit took Elton to the changing-room and gave him a red shirt and white shorts with a red stripe down the side.

"Those should fit," he said.

Gershwin was panting and gazing eagerly at Cluff. The manager thought he looked a bit left out of things and rummaged through a basket until he found a red and white rosette which had "Woofits are Wizard" on it.

He fixed it to Gershwin's collar.

"There! Now you are a Woofits player too," he said.

The dog jumped excitedly, hitting Cluff on the nose. Cluff laughed and rumpled his ears.

When they got home, Elton's dad, John Willy Woofit, was polishing his trombone. He played in the brass band that entertained the crowd at the Cup Final.

Elton told him about meeting Mr Cluff Woofit and how he and Gershwin were to be team mascots.

"Humph!" said John Willy Woofit. "Best playing on Saturday will be at half-time."

He gave one or two more rubs with the duster and checked if he could see his face in the shiny metal.

He could.

Angela Woofit, Elton's sister, was practising her elocution. (She wanted to be a newsreader.)

"Oh, our Elton is a proper mess," she said, without even looking up from her book.

"No, he's not. He's lovely," said Elton's mother, without looking up either. She was knitting Elton a scarf to wear at the Final.

"Oh, come on, Gershwin!" said Elton in disgust, and they went upstairs to Elton's bedroom.

Elton played his guitar for a while, dreaming of being a pop-singing soccer star.

Gershwin dozed off and dreamed of playing football with his nose and chasing cats.

On the day of the Final, the whole village was busy. It was a mining village. The football ground, which was near the pit, was steadily filling up.

The Cloggers' supporters wore blue and yellow scarves and rosettes, and The Woofits' fans were dressed in red and white.

The sergeant from the Police Station met The Cloggers team as they arrived at the ground.

"Welcome, gentlemen," he said, his moustache quivering with importance as the team left the bus.

"I'm Sergeant Fox – not to be confused with box, cox or sox."

He started to laugh. He always laughed at his own jokes. This was his favourite.

The Cloggers team looked at him in stony silence. They were too nervous to laugh.

"Well, may the best team win!" said the sergeant, looking serious again.

"So long as it's The Woofits," he added under his breath.

In the dressing-room, Cluff Woofit was giving his last minute instructions to the players.

"You might not be the greatest players in the world, but you have the greatest manager," he said. "Now, watch out for Skinner Clogger. He's the best they've got – and he's not particular who he kicks."

There was a great roar from the crowd when the two teams went on the pitch.

Elton felt very proud because he was allowed to lead The Woofits into the middle where he was introduced to Georgie Woofit and Skinner Clogger, the two captains.

Skinner was the biggest man Elton had ever seen. He had legs like tree trunks and eyes like slits.

"I wouldn't like to play against him," thought Elton.

How right he was! After ten minutes, Skinner had shoulder-charged one of The Woofits so hard that he disappeared over the barrier into the crowd.

When the player woke up several minutes later, he was in the dressing-room and another player had taken his place.

At half-time, Elton sat in the dressing-room with Gershwin while Cluff Woofit gave a pep talk.

"Not good enough! Not enough effort. You're all scared of Skinner," he said.

"I'm not," said Elton.

"I'll remember that," said Cluff.

In the second half, things looked really bad for The Woofits.

The dreaded Skinner had the game by the scruff of the neck – as well as one or two players!

Cluff Woofit was getting very cross.

"Right, Elton," he said. "Here's your big chance. I'm taking a player off and putting you on."

"This really is my big chance," said Elton to Gershwin, who wagged his tail.

"Look! They're putting on midgets, now," said Skinner when Elton ran on to the pitch.

There were only ten minutes left to play when Elton first got the ball.

He looked about him to see who to pass it to and was about to kick it to Georgie Woofit when he was knocked to the floor.

The next thing he knew, he was being licked on the face by a worried-looking Gershwin.

"What happened?" he asked.

"Skinner ran over you," said Mr Cluff. "You mustn't dwell on the ball, lad, with the likes of him around."

For a while Elton felt very groggy. So did the team. With three minutes of the game left there was no score, but The Cloggers were becoming more and more confident.

Then Georgie Woofit passed the ball to Elton, who was standing on the halfway line.

Elton had no sooner got the ball than he was flattened again by the awful Skinner.

The Woofits crowd booed, but the referee did nothing.

It was all too much for the loyal Gershwin.

As Skinner strode downfield towards The Woofits' goal, Gershwin raced on to the field and headed towards him.

And surprise for Skinner! Just at the moment when he was preparing to score a goal, the ball was whisked from his feet by a dog wearing a Woofits rosette!

With the ball at his nose, Gershwin set off upfield towards The Cloggers' goal. Every time a Clogger player tried to stop him, he flicked the ball past him and left him kicking the air.

Elton wondered if he should call Gershwin off – or if Gershwin *would* be called off.

The crowd was going wild.

"Oh, dear! Mr Cluff's going to be mad at me," thought Elton.

"Heel!" he shouted to Gershwin.

But Gershwin was deaf to all commands. All that mattered to him was the ball. Thrilled by the roars of the crowd, he left player after player flat on his back.

But at last he began to feel tired. He nosed the ball over to Elton and sat gazing hopefully up at his master.

"Shoot, Elton, lad! Shoot!" cried Mr Cluff.

With a start, Elton realised that he was standing in front of The Cloggers' goal, with only the keeper to beat. The roar of the crowd was in his ears and he could see the goalkeeper jumping up and down with excitement.

Elton had never felt so nervous in his life. Skinner was racing down the field towards him. He closed his eyes and kicked the ball.

When he opened them again, the ball was in the net.

Gershwin was chasing his tail and the supporters were yelling.

The referee pointed to the middle and then blew his whistle.

Elton had scored the winning goal with the last kick of the game!

The Cloggers were disgusted.
"How can a dog play for a team?" asked Skinner, who was very fed up.

"He belongs to the club – that's why he can play for us," said Uncle Athelstone Woofit, (who just happened to be the referee).

"In any case, it wasn't the dog that scored. It was our Elton."

And, of course, the referee's word is final.

Later, Cluff Woofit spoke to the TV reporters.

"I decided to play the dog to upset the rhythm of their defence," he said.

Gershwin gave him a funny look.

That night, at the celebration dinner, Elton was given the place of honour.

Elton's mum watched it live on television.

"Our Elton's a clever lad," she said, knitting furiously.

She still hadn't finished Elton's scarf.

"I think he's a twit," said Angela Woofit, jealous because Elton was on television and she wasn't.

"He'll do," was all Mr Woofit said, but secretly he was very proud.

Gershwin slept on the rug in front of the fire. He was tired out after the game – but he had a super dream – all about scoring goals and chasing rabbits.

As seen on ITV
With acknowledgment to
TRIDENT TELEVISION LIMITED
ISBN 0 00 123528 1

Printed in Great Britain.